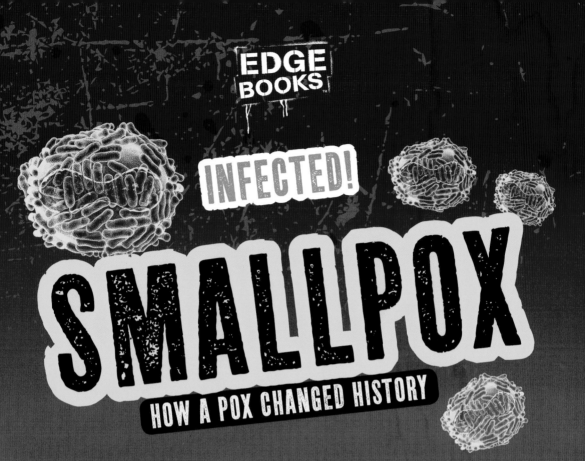

EDGE BOOKS™

INFECTED!

SMALLPOX

HOW A POX CHANGED HISTORY

by Janie Havemeyer

Consultant

Sharon Medcalf, PhD
Director, Center for Biosecurity, Biopreparedness,
and Emerging Infectious Diseases
University of Nebraska Medical Center

CAPSTONE PRESS
a capstone imprint

Edge Books are published by Capstone Press,
1710 Roe Crest Drive, North Mankato, Minnesota 56003
www.mycapstone.com

Library of Congress Cataloging-in-Publication Data
Names: Havemeyer, Janie, author.
Title: Smallpox : how a pox changed history / by Janie Havemeyer.
Description: North Mankato, Minnesota : Capstone Press, [2019] | Series:
   Infected! | «Edge Books are published by Capstone Press.» | Audience: Ages
   8-14. | Audience: Grades 4 to 6. | Includes bibliographical references and
   index.
Identifiers: LCCN 2018036904 (print) | LCCN 2018037291 (ebook) | ISBN
   9781543555141 (ebook) | ISBN 9781543555028 (hardcover : alk. paper)
Subjects: LCSH: Smallpox--Juvenile literature. |
   Smallpox--Prevention--Juvenile literature. | Diseases and
   history--Juvenile literature.
Classification: LCC QR201.S6 (ebook) | LCC QR201.S6 H38 2019 (print) | DDC
   616.9/12--dc23
LC record available at https://lccn.loc.gov/2018036904

Editorial Credits
Editor: Maddie Spalding
Designer: Craig Hinton
Production Specialist: Ryan Gale

Quote Sources
p. 4, Howard W. Haggard, *From Medicine Man to Doctor: The Story of the Science of Healing.* Mineola, N.Y.: Dover Publications, 2004; p. 20, Stefan Riedel, "Edward Jenner and the History of Smallpox and Vaccination." *Baylor University Medical Center,* January 2005

Photo Credits
Alamy: Marion Kaplan, 25, Trinity Mirror/Mirrorpix, 26; Defense Visual Information Distribution Service: Petty Officer 2nd Class Ashante Hammons, 28–29; Getty Images: Patrick Landmann/Getty Images News, 13; National Archives Catalog: Russell Lee, cover (people); Newscom: BSIP/Photoshot, 8, UPPA/Photoshot, 17; North Wind Picture Archives: 14; Shutterstock Images: chrisdorney, 21, Everett Historical, 7, 11, 19, 23, Everett-Art, 5, Kateryna Kon, cover (virus)

Design Elements
Shutterstock Images: ilolab

Printed in the United States of America.
PA48

TABLE OF CONTENTS

CHAPTER 1

THE DEADLY POX

On December 20, 1694, Queen Mary II of England collapsed. Flashes of pain ran through her head and down her back. She sometimes felt chilly, which caused her to shiver. At other times she sweated. Hundreds of people in London, England, were coming down with a deadly disease called smallpox. A historian at the time wrote, "Smallpox was always present, filling the churchyard with corpses." Queen Mary was afraid she had come down with smallpox. She shut herself in her room at Kensington Palace. She did not want the disease to spread.

Three days later a reddish-purple color spread across Mary's face. Nine doctors gathered by her bedside. Based on Mary's **symptoms**, they thought the disease could be either measles or smallpox.

symptom—a change in a person's body or mind that is a sign of a disease

Measles is an infection that causes people to break out in rashes. Doctors hoped the disease was measles and not smallpox. Smallpox was deadlier than measles. The doctors had to wait until Mary developed more symptoms to find out which disease she had.

FAST FACT

The smallpox virus spread very easily. People could catch it when a nearby sick person sneezed or coughed. If people breathed the air around a sick person, they could get the virus.

Mary II was the queen of England from 1689 to 1694.

The next day blisters formed on Mary's face, arms, hands, and feet. The doctors agreed this was smallpox. But they did not know whether Mary had a deadly form of the disease.

Doctors typically tried a few treatments on people with smallpox. One common treatment was wrapping the patient in blankets in a hot room. Doctors thought this would help the patient sweat out the disease. Some doctors tried bloodletting. This involved draining blood out of a patient's body. Historical accounts do not explain the type of treatment Mary received.

Mary's health soon worsened. Her blisters flattened and spread into red sores along her body. The sores turned purple and black. Red rings formed around each one. Later the sores filled with blood. The queen gasped for breath. She spit up blood.

Mary had a rare form of smallpox called hemorrhagic smallpox. This was the deadliest type of smallpox. Victims bled out from openings in the body. Mary bled from her nose, eyes, and skin. She could no longer eat, drink, or speak. Eight days after her first symptoms, Mary died.

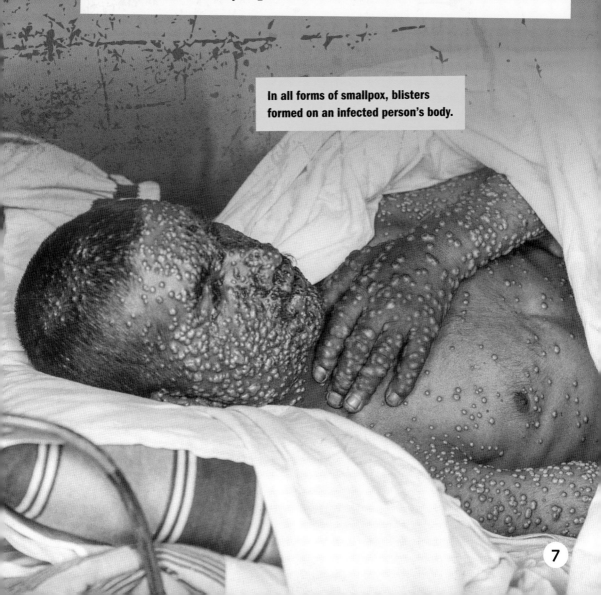

In all forms of smallpox, blisters formed on an infected person's body.

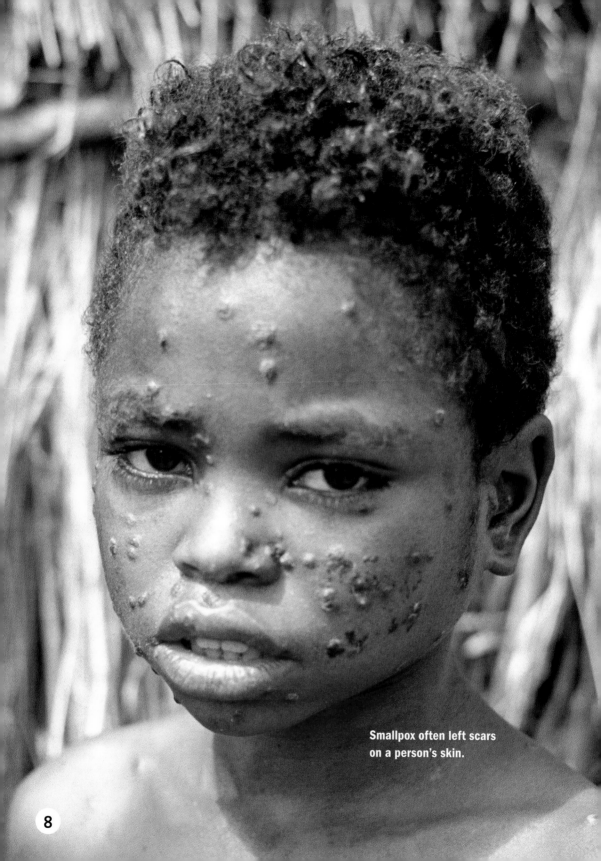

Smallpox often left scars on a person's skin.

WHAT WAS SMALLPOX?

Smallpox was one of the world's deadliest diseases. About three out of every ten people who got it died. Smallpox was **eradicated**, or eliminated worldwide, in 1980. But before then the disease had killed hundreds of millions of people.

A **virus** infected people with smallpox. A virus is something that invades a person's body. Once in the body, it attacks a person's cells. The virus then multiplies, causing sickness. Two types of viruses caused smallpox. The variola minor virus caused a mild form of smallpox. People who caught this virus would usually have fevers, headaches, and backaches. They would develop rashes. Later bumps called lesions would break out on their skin. The infected person would usually recover within a few weeks. Only about 1 percent of people died from this type of smallpox.

eradicate—to completely eliminate something, such as a disease
virus— a germ that can only grow and reproduce inside the living cells of other organisms

The variola major virus was deadlier and more common than the variola minor virus. Its symptoms included fevers, headaches, backaches, and vomiting. A rash developed about four days after the first symptoms. Then the victim's skin would break out in lesions. The lesions would turn into blisters. About 30 percent of infected people died from this type of smallpox. People usually died within 10 to 16 days after their symptoms first appeared. Hemorrhagic smallpox was a type of variola major smallpox. People with hemorrhagic smallpox often died five or six days after getting a rash.

FAST FACT

Another name for smallpox was "the speckled monster." This is because it covered a person's body in blisters and sores.

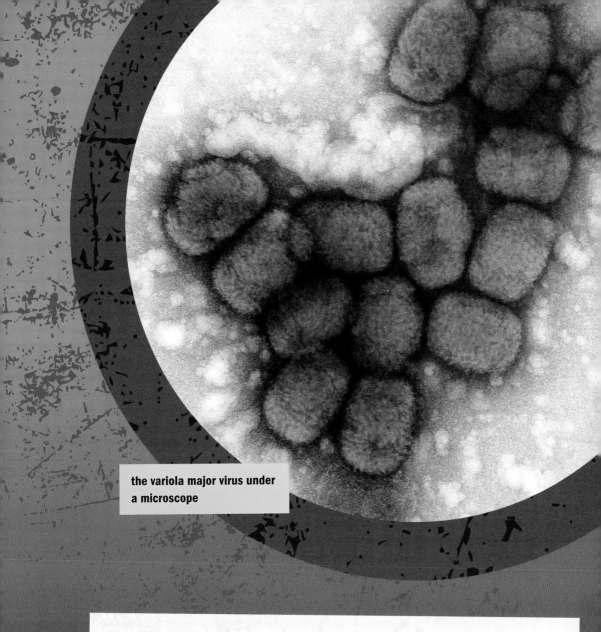

the variola major virus under
a microscope

People who survived smallpox had permanent
damage. They had pockmarks, or big pits, on
their skin. These were scars that disfigured a
person's skin. Some people even went blind.

CHAPTER 2

THE HISTORY OF SMALLPOX

Historians believe the first smallpox **epidemic** occurred in Egypt in 1350 BC. Historians are not sure how many people died from this epidemic. Some people think the Egyptian pharaoh Ramses V died of smallpox in 1157 BC. The Egyptians preserved the bodies of their pharaohs, including Ramses V. Scars on Ramses V's face are still visible today. They look like smallpox scars.

FAST FACT

Among people who were never exposed to smallpox, the death rate could be as high as nine in 10 people.

epidemic—an outbreak of a disease that affects many people within a particular region

THE SMALLPOX PANDEMIC

Smallpox spread around the world for thousands of years. When a disease spreads all over the world, it is called a **pandemic**. By AD 1000 only a few regions had not been infected by smallpox. It had not spread to Russia, Scandinavia, Iceland, North America, or South America. People who lived in infected regions, including Europeans, developed some resistance to the virus.

Pharaoh Ramses V may have died from smallpox.

pandemic—an outbreak of a disease that spreads across several countries or continents and affects many people

European settlers brought the disease to the unaffected regions. People in these regions had never been exposed to smallpox. This meant that their bodies did not know how to fight the virus.

In 1241 a Danish ship brought smallpox to Iceland. The disease killed nearly half of the country's population. In April 1520 a slave from Africa being held captive on a Spanish ship came down with smallpox. The ship docked in Mexico, and the virus spread throughout the region. About 90 percent of Mexico's population died from smallpox.

Smallpox killed many people in the Wampanoag tribe in Massachusetts in the 1600s.

SMALLPOX IN NORTH AMERICA

In the 1600s Dutch, English, and French settlers built **colonies** in North America. They also brought smallpox to the region. Thousands of Native Americans died from smallpox. The disease almost wiped out the Algonquin and Narragansett tribes in 1616. Settlers traveled in North America to trade goods, spreading smallpox throughout the region. In 1639 the disease killed about half of the 20,000 members of the Huron-Wendat community.

RED TREATMENT

The color red was once thought to have special healing powers. It was used to treat smallpox patients beginning in the 1200s. People who had smallpox slept in red bedsheets and wore red nightclothes. They thought the red cloth would warm their skin so they could sweat out the infection. In the early 1900s, a Danish doctor used red lights to try to heal smallpox patients. He called it the "red treatment." He shone the light on smallpox patients. The red treatment did not work. But doctors kept using this treatment until 1920.

colony—an area controlled by another country

CHAPTER 3

SMALLPOX EXPERIMENTS

Early in the disease's history, people began to notice that no one got smallpox twice. In about 1550 Chinese doctors used this knowledge to try to fight smallpox. They crushed smallpox scabs into a powder. Then they blew it up a patient's nose. The patient would get a mild form of smallpox but usually recovered. This method was called **variolation**. People in China, Arabia, and Africa began to use this method.

LADY MONTAGU

Many doctors in Europe thought variolation was a crazy idea. But an English woman named Lady Mary Wortley Montagu changed their minds. In 1721 an outbreak of smallpox struck London.

variolation—the method of giving someone smallpox to prevent them from getting the disease a second time

Montagu had visited the city of Constantinople in present-day Istanbul, Turkey. She saw doctors variolating people there. She asked her doctor, Charles Maitland, to variolate her son and daughter. Maitland was not against variolation, so he did as she asked. Montagu's children did not come down with smallpox. This persuaded more doctors in Europe to try variolation.

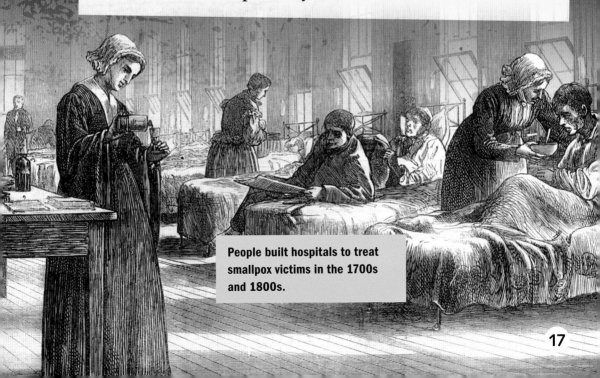

People built hospitals to treat smallpox victims in the 1700s and 1800s.

A BOSTON EXPERIMENT

In 1721 a smallpox epidemic broke out in Boston, Massachusetts. A preacher named Cotton Mather urged doctors to try variolation. Mather had heard about variolation from an African man he enslaved. The man's name was Onesimus. He had seen how variolation could help prevent smallpox.

Mather persuaded a doctor named Zabdiel Boylston to test the variolation method. Boylston used blister fluid from mild cases of smallpox to infect 281 patients. He placed the blister fluid on cuts on his patients' skin. Six of these patients died. The rest recovered. They did not get smallpox a second time.

FAST FACT
People who were infected by smallpox were kept apart from healthy people. This was to help keep the disease from spreading.

About 5,980 people got smallpox during the epidemic in Boston. Of those infected, 844 died. Variolation helped saved some people's lives.

A FAILED INVASION

In 1779 smallpox saved England from being invaded. A fleet of French and Spanish ships gathered in the English Channel. They prepared to attack England. The French fleet was made up of about 400,000 men. An outbreak of smallpox struck soldiers on board the French ships. More than half of the men came down with smallpox. Hundreds died. The Spanish and French troops did not have enough men to attack. They were forced to retreat.

Cotton Mather supported the variolation method to prevent smallpox.

CHAPTER 4

DEVELOPING A VACCINE

Doctors continued to study smallpox throughout the 1700s. Edward Jenner was an English doctor in the late 1700s. He once heard a milkmaid say, "I shall never have smallpox for I have had cowpox." Cowpox is a mild illness that sometimes affects cows. The disease is related to smallpox but is not deadly. Infected cows develop sores on their udders. The sores are full of **pus**. But the cows tend to recover quickly.

Milkmaids often caught cowpox when they milked infected cows. But they did not get smallpox after being infected with cowpox. They believed that cowpox protected them from smallpox. Jenner wanted to study this to prove if it was true.

pus—a thick, yellowish fluid that is produced when part of a person's or animal's body becomes infected

A statue in London, England, honors doctor Edward Jenner, who developed the smallpox vaccine in the late 1700s.

COWPOX EXPERIMENTS

In 1796 Jenner treated a milkmaid who had blisters on her hand. Jenner **diagnosed** the blisters as cowpox. He removed some of the pus from the blisters. He then used it to infect an eight-year-old boy named James Phipps. Jenner made two cuts on the boy's arm and rubbed the pus in. James soon came down with cowpox. But he was better within a week. Jenner later tried to give James a mild form of smallpox. But James never got smallpox. This was an important first step in proving that cowpox could help prevent smallpox. It was also the first step in developing a smallpox **vaccine**.

CONTROLLING SMALLPOX

Jenner did more studies. He proved that cowpox protected people from smallpox. This method of using a virus to protect against disease is called **vaccination**.

diagnose—to identify a disease from certain symptoms
vaccine—a substance made up of dead, weakened, or living organisms that is injected into a person to protect against a disease
vaccination—the method of using a substance made up of dead, weakened, or living organisms to protect against a disease

After Jenner published his findings in 1798, the number of vaccinations increased. Vaccination was much safer that variolation. Vaccination had a lower death rate than variolation.

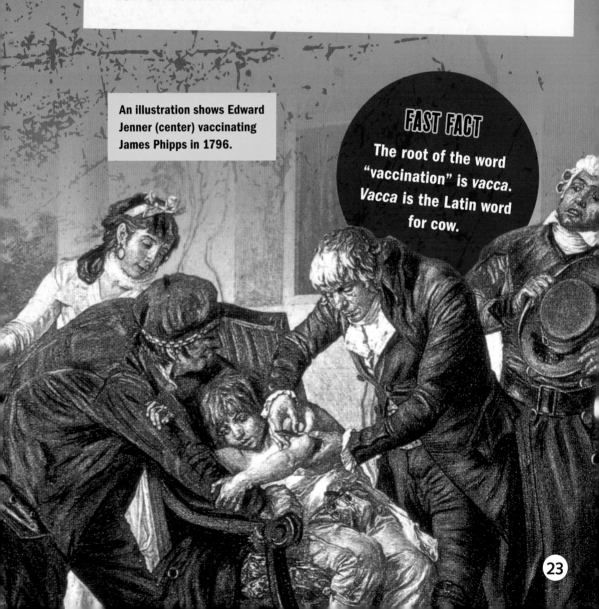

An illustration shows Edward Jenner (center) vaccinating James Phipps in 1796.

FAST FACT

The root of the word "vaccination" is vacca. Vacca is the Latin word for cow.

CHAPTER 5

ELIMINATING SMALLPOX

The smallpox vaccination reduced the number of people who got smallpox. But some people refused to be vaccinated. They thought the vaccination was unsafe.

In March 1947 a few cases of smallpox broke out in New York City. Two people died from the disease. The mayor of New York City urged all New Yorkers to get vaccinations. His efforts were successful. About 5 to 6 million people got vaccinations. That was about 64 to 77 percent of the total population in New York City at the time.

In 1966 the World Health Organization (WHO) began a campaign to eradicate smallpox in 10 years. From 1967 to 1977, WHO teams traveled all over the world to find smallpox cases. They set out to vaccinate 80 percent of the people in every country. They offered rewards for anyone who reported smallpox cases. When a case was reported, WHO workers separated the patient from healthy people. They vaccinated everyone who had been in contact with the patient. This helped stop the spread of the disease.

An Ethiopian woman receives a smallpox check and vaccination in 1976.

In 1977 a few cases of smallpox broke out in Somalia. After those cases were treated, one year passed without any reported cases. It looked as though the WHO had accomplished its goal.

A NEW TWIST

In 1978 two new cases of smallpox occurred in England. One of the victims was medical photographer Janet Parker. Parker worked at the University of Birmingham in Birmingham, England.

People line up to receive smallpox vaccinations after Janet Parker was infected with the disease in 1978.

PUBLIC HE
DEPART
IMMUNISA
SECTION

A sample of the variola major virus was stored in a laboratory one floor below where Parker worked. Doctors believed the virus moved up an airshaft. Parker probably breathed it in. She also spread the disease to her mother. Parker's mother survived, but Parker did not.

Parker and her mother were the last known victims of smallpox. After Parker's death, the WHO asked all countries to either destroy their smallpox samples or send them to two official WHO locations. These WHO locations were in Atlanta, Georgia, and Moscow, Russia. The samples were locked up in safes. The WHO decided to save these samples until leaders around the world could agree on whether to destroy or save them.

THE SMALLPOX VIRUS TODAY

In May 1980 the WHO made an announcement. The organization said that smallpox had been eradicated. But frozen tubes of the virus are still kept in storage safes around the world. Today the debate continues on whether these tubes should be stored or destroyed. Some scientists think the samples could help researchers learn more about the disease. They think the samples could help people test better smallpox vaccines. Other scientists think the smallpox virus could be used to fight other viruses, such as the human immunodeficiency virus (HIV). But many people think it is too dangerous to keep the samples. They worry that the samples could be stolen and used as a weapon. For now the smallpox virus lives on.

Today only certain people receive the smallpox vaccine, such as members of the U.S. armed forces.

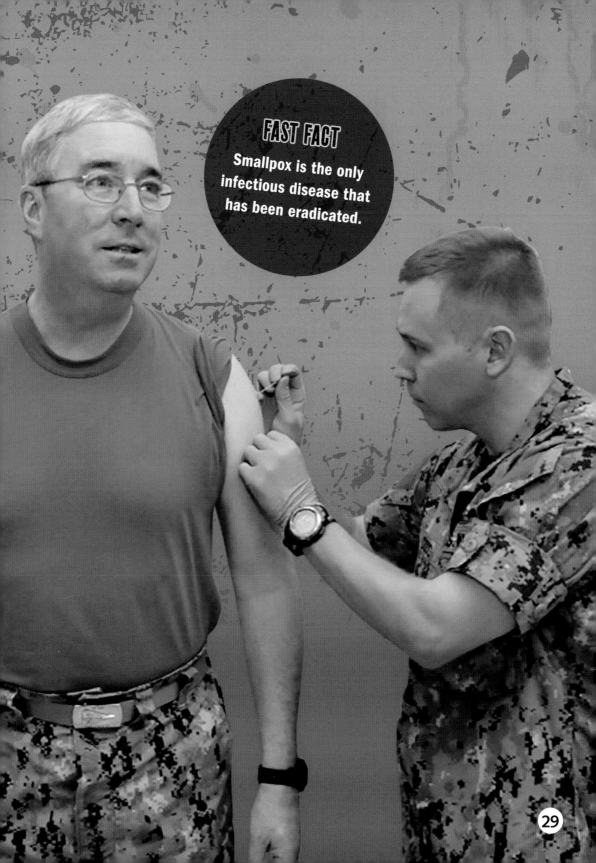

FAST FACT

Smallpox is the only infectious disease that has been eradicated.

GLOSSARY

colony (KAHL-uh-nee)—an area controlled by another country

diagnose (dy-ig-NOHS)—to identify a disease from certain symptoms

epidemic (eh-pih-DEH-mik)—an outbreak of a disease that affects many people within a particular region

eradicate (eh-RAH-dih-kate)—to completely eliminate something, such as a disease

pandemic (pan-DEH-mik)—an outbreak of a disease that spreads across several countries or continents and affects many people

pus (PUHSS)—a thick, yellowish fluid that is produced when part of a person's or animal's body becomes infected

symptom (SIM-tuhm)—a change in a person's body or mind that is a sign of a disease

vaccination (vak-suh-NAY-shuhn)—the method of using a substance made up of dead, weakened, or living organisms to protect against a disease

vaccine (vak-SEEN)—a substance made up of dead, weakened, or living organisms that is injected into a person to protect against a disease

variolation (ver-ee-oh-LAY-shuhn)—the method of giving someone smallpox to prevent them from getting the disease a second time

virus (VY-ruhss)—a germ that can only grow and reproduce inside the living cells of other organisms

READ MORE

Andrews, Lawrence. *Smallpox*. Deadliest Diseases of All Time. New York: Cavendish Square Publishing, 2015.

Markovics, Joyce L. *Tiny Invaders!: Deadly Microorganisms*. Nature's Invaders. North Mankato, Minn.: Capstone Press, 2014.

Shea, John M. *Viruses Up Close*. Under the Microscope. New York: Gareth Stevens Publishing, 2014.

INTERNET SITES

Use FactHound to find Internet sites related to this book.

Visit www.facthound.com

Just type in 9781543555028 and go.

 Check out projects, games and lots more at
www.capstonekids.com

INDEX